A Map for Exiting the Body

A Map for Exiting the Body

Jin Cordaro

Terrapin Books

© 2025 by Jin Cordaro
Printed in the United States of America.
All rights reserved.
No part of this book may be reproduced in any manner, except for brief quotations embodied in critical articles or reviews.

Terrapin Books
4 Midvale Avenue
West Caldwell, NJ 07006

www.terrapinbooks.com

ISBN: 978-1-947896-79-6
Library of Congress Control Number: 2024951868

First Edition

Cover art: *Nature's First Green Is Gold*
by Amy Salomone

for Lou, Izzy, and Liv
—thank you for all your gifts, including time

Contents

Sometimes in the Country of Ourselves   3

1
All Your Lives, Your Sister
    and You Wore Long Braids   7
A Test for Depression   8
Dear Ross Gay: About   10
Your Book on Finding Delight   10
What's in the Blood   12
I Was Born in a Room with Only Four Seats   14
Broken Umbrella Song   16

2
Once There Was a Woman
    Who Could Only Say *I'm Sorry*   19
Hunting in the Cellar, in the Middle
    of the Afternoon   21
Acerbic You Does Not Like Laid Back You   22
What You Found in Your Shed Yesterday   24
When I Go Too Long
    Without Reading a Poem   26
That Time You Stole
    Someone's Shopping Cart   27
Lust   28

3
My Husband Is Burning   31
Sonnet for a Husband   32
Why I Lose Rings   33
How to Divide One Whole You   34
My Life in a Purse   36

4

When We Come Back to Town,
  We Come Back to the Body   41
Observing the Narcissist in Its Natural Habitat   42
Homemade Dress, 1971   43
A Revisionist's Dream of Ice Cream   44
Eating My Korean   45
Flavor Is in the Hands   47

5

I Go Back to the Night I Was Named   51
Lessons in Chess   52
What You Learn to Say in French   54
Driving Lessons for Girls   55
He Said He Knew of a Place
  Where We Could Swim   57
How Much to Cut   58
Every Morning, I Slip My Feet into My Feet   59
As You Drive by the Cornfield
  on County Road 522   60

6

A Poem for No One   65
You've been dreaming
  about street lamps again   67
In the Kingdom of Obsolete Things   68
This Morning, While Washing the Dishes   70
How Best to See the Stars at Night   71
Ways to Be Buried in the Movies   73
After We Buried the Dog in the Dark   75

Acknowledgments   77
About the Author   79

*Not until we are lost do we begin
to understand ourselves.*

—Henry David Thoreau

Sometimes in the Country of Ourselves

We drive through the towns of our mistakes,
no idea what road we've gotten on,
long past where we wanted to turn
so we backtrack
only to find the thick barreled trunk of
a choice we made fallen across the road.
We make a map, locate ourselves,
look for an alternate route but then,
we get a flat—
precarious and out of balance,
no sign of an exit ramp for miles.
No way to leave ourselves,

we drive in circles,
passing the same conflicts
the same words like landmarks, the same people,
foundations still cemented in our memory,
bearing damage from whatever weather
they've endured. Torn shingles, rotted self-esteem.
No more load-bearing wall.
An old church in need of paint.
and a bigger congregation.

Sometimes too
we drive through the town of our ambition
to see if the future is written yet

across the lit-up billboard with a coming soon sign,
only to find
the empty lot now choked with weeds,
unrecognizable,
sown over with unintended seeds.

We go to the country of Ourselves
while washing the dishes,
while waiting for sleep in the dark,
looking to find one small shelter of purpose,
where the past no longer beats down hot
on our neck,
where the future is round and full,
riding low in the sky.
Bright enough to see by.

All Your Lives, Your Sister and You Wore Long Braids

Then your sister turns 16, and can strike the ball
across the tennis court—harder
than your parents could ever strike either of you.

Her body rears up like a horse that knows
it can leap the fence. You see it's true.
You see it when her feet churn the clay surface
of the court, and the muscles of her thighs
shake like a tremor in the earth, like
a hand reaching up to stop another hand.

When she cuts her braid, you see her
wearing the skin of a horse beneath her clothes.

She begins to appear in your dreams,
summoned like an unfulfilled wish,
pacing the same length of fence,
showing you where the ground slopes,
and the one rail is just low enough.

A Test for Depression

Severity is measured by: the number of days
since your hope was last seen, how often

you try to repeat the motions of joy,
your resiliency divided by inertia,

a gradient scale of desire.
Warning! Please note before combining

with any other illness: call your doctor
if you begin to disappear,

if it turns your dreams into a sorrow factory,
those driven with fire carry antibodies,

may cause imbalance on the thin line
between character and disease.

Some of the leading causes of depression are:
a joy-sucking machine someone has installed

below your heart. a constant inadequate diet
lacking in forgiveness, prolonged immersion

in hot regret, your mother's personality
still hanging in the closet.

Your depression is:
an eternal houseguest who keeps you up

most nights, a pet who chews on your life
more than half the days, a wail

that your cells sing in unison—
you are their organ sometimes,

the symptom of a symptom
of another affliction.

Dear Ross Gay: About Your Book on Finding Delight

What if joy requires a gene cluster
of overly sensitive receptors to be shut off
to stop the excessive taste of bitters
in your memories?

What if sorrow is a deficiency
of rods and cones meant to see the shape of joy
laid out in colored mosaic—
a test for joy. For others sharp and distinct
but for you just one flat monochrome.
You can never see what's spelled out.

And what if your tympanic membrane
were a loosened drumskin—
unable to transmit the vibrations of joy.
Turnkeys to bring the skin back to taut
and vibrant sound long ago broken off or
missing. Does your book include instructions
for repair?

You say joy needs sorrow to exist.
Then depression would be a windfall,
a lottery jackpot. I'd like to participate
in this fantasy that we are repairable
by overabundance:
a high dose of flowers growing by the curb

and high fives from strangers
enough to compensate for generations
of inherited trauma bulging in a vein.
But I know better.

Please provide instructions on
how to will your genes to change, to achieve
an epigenetic miracle.
Tell us how to clip the sections
full of cracked eggs and shadows.
How to build rung by rung
a gene segment full of birds
doing as they please in the girders of an airport,
fireflies lighting the way at night.

What's in the Blood

The way we walk is in the blood.
Heels dug in with purpose,
some a hitch in the hip, others light and quick
leaving the least footprint possible.
We try to run from death that's in the blood—
the date and manner written like
a constellation, laid out in bright dots,
mile markers on the way.
Canis major—following Orion
it runs the endless loop of body.
We picture it obedient,
never asking why or where it goes
until the body can no longer go.
It carries the cells
of mother to child and
child to mother.

But blood is fate. Blood is our story.
Both memories and lies we tell—
who is the problem,
who is to blame.
In truth there are two parts to blood.
It can boil or run cold,
both dark and light,
anger and patience,
cruelty and generosity.

Two dogs wrestling inside of us,
one on top, they pin and reverse.
No sight of who will ever win—
who will forgive the other first.

I Was Born in a Room
with Only Four Seats

And eight children,
on a secondhand couch reupholstered.
I was the curtains closed during the day, and
the one small brass lamp on at night.

I was the surge of a sewing machine
whirring late into the night and
the inflamed knot in my mother's knuckle.
I was the clouds growing over my father's eyes,
the small red spots of heat rash on his legs.

I was fermented cabbage brined in red pepper.
I was soybean paste mixed with resentment—
my mother shaped and mounded me then
dried and strung me up from the rafters.
I was made by my mother's hands.

I was a discarded box of scraps
resembling triangles and squares,
survival sewn together—
I was the leftover ideas my parents held onto,
Someday you'll come into use.

I was the gear turning over and over
in silence without laughter.
I was the monotonous wheel,
waiting to spin free.

Broken Umbrella Song

We felt the rib snap, and
the low hum began
in the backs of our throats, no, deeper
in our chests like small alarms buzzing.
The neighbors kept on swinging,
kept jumping off in midair because
the song of regret was not their song.

So we waited until they went inside; then
we carried it like a broken bird and prayed
for metal to heal as bone.
And when it didn't, we prayed again,
for a place deep like a well, because
we knew how this song would end.
Shame is a permanent flinch,
a thing that animals will bury.

This is the song for all the things we never intend.
This is the tune for all the things
that can never be undone.

2

Once There Was a Woman Who Could Only Say I'm Sorry

When the man at the deli counter calls her up,
she tries to say, *Salami please*
but instead it comes out, *I'm sorry.*
So she points which works just fine until
he asks, *How much?*
One pound comes out the same,
I'm sorry,

as she stumbles backwards
into how to get what she needs,
while the man leans forward
into how to give her what she wants
because misunderstanding is either
a step-on-your-toes kind of dance,
or a barely touch kind of dance—
a bubble around you kind of dance
and nobody can come in.

Then she holds up one finger
so they both come back to the salami
and he asks, *Just one pound?* Too much
to eat before it spoils but
no way to indicate a half
So she nods, and he asks, *Anything else?*
But she's too tired to dance all over again
just for some cheese, *I'm sorry.*

She raises her hand to indicate thanks.
He winks and says, *Come back next week,
the roast beef is on sale.*
She nods and thinks,
I'd rather burn this whole place down.

Hunting in the Cellar,
in the Middle of the Afternoon

We caught the mice,
stepped on their tails while they ran and ran.
Resented what they took and left behind.
We copied the grown-ups.

Stepped on their tails to make them run,
wagged our fingers at them.
We played grown-up.
Made them obey.

Wagged our fingers at them.
Dragged them screaming into the woods,
taught them to obey.
We were formed.

Dragged them screaming into the woods,
flung them down into the dirt.
We were formed one way, not even
when we aspired to be different.

We flung them down into the dirt,
knowing they would not come back.
Even when we aspired to be different,
we remained the same.

-

Acerbic You Does Not Like Laid Back You

Acerbic You and Laid Back You were conjoined
from birth, two halves of a heart and
a lifetime battle of who controls the muscles,
who controls the nerves,
who will make the bones dance.

Acerbic You controls the ribs,
protects the heart from people
who accelerate at a lane merge,
calls out people who cut the line and
thanks people who don't hold the door.
And Ascerbic You controls the skin,
shields the insides from the whipping sting
of insults and selfishness.
Holds you all together.

Laid Back You controls the stomach
muscles that know the quiver of good news.
The duality of clench and release, inhale and exhale,
the mouth, the pleasure of sweet
and savory, cravings for variety and impulse.
And Laid Back You controls
the reproductive organs, the queen of pleasure,
of everything that can clench and release.

Ascerbic You wants to keep the vessels tight
when it's cold, keeping what's important
at the core, while Laid Back You wants
the vessels open to warm the body,
drive what's needed to the farthest corners.
One half pulls it close, survives,
the other half pushes out,
preserves the soul.

Ascerbic You wants to separate
from Laid Back You,
but dividing property would be a bitch.
Who would get the hands?
Who would survive
with half a heart?

What You Found in Your Shed Yesterday

Was an entire galaxy swirling above the tractor,
worn out and leaking stars.
It contained everyone you know,
held them close enough to see their valleys,
see them move on their own ellipse.
You had come to fill the lawnmower,
gas can now lost behind
whole planets made of the dust of disappointment
swirling gas clouds of wanting more, and
your life a universe of bodies who can never reach.
Then you too were a moon
in the corner weightless and singular—
searching for other moons.
But the darkness always expands.
You tried to blow some out but
it grew and followed you—
a dark cloud over your desk
at work; the phone would ring;
at the other end, a steady pulse, a signal.
it followed you outside the car,
swallowed you until you got lost—
missed your street,
took a left down the wrong memory.
Roads which led to more dust and swirling gas.

And as you drove through your life,
you were no longer a moon.
You were a white dwarf star burned out,
imploding from the weight.

When I Go Too Long Without Reading a Poem

I think only of how
they would stroke my head
in the evening if they were here.
At night, in my sleep, I whimper
for their solace, the scent of them
fading. I sit by the window to see
when they are coming,
if they are coming—
a craving greater than food now.
I pace at the door.
The tail of my grief curls under me.
I become inconsolable, alone
with nothing to hold close
to my chest and feel
as if I am understood.

That Time You Stole Someone's Shopping Cart

With their shopping list in the seat,
and a flower doodled in the corner—a sign,
not a curse or a prayer, a devotion,
a singular language
to nourish and be nourished by.

Familiar words, combined in a cipher,
you can only translate every third word—
paprika followed by shallots means
to put effort into caring.
Cranberries combined with pecans
and butternut squash means
to sustain, keep well.

What would this taste like?
This list a thin opaque crepe filled with
the soft, oozing breadth of someone's attention and time.
You slip it into your jacket,
keep your hand in your pocket as you walk the store.
Rush home to unfold it, imagine it still warm
slightly browned on a skillet,
sweet and bready with love.
You chew it slowly—
the only piece of food to be found.

Lust

You'll want to drizzle rich black sesame oil over everything.
You'll want things spicy and pickled, with tiny whole fish, when
normally you never eat things with the head or eyes.
You'll take your dumplings in any shape or form.
With a thin, transparent skin, or a hard, fried shell.
You'll want your noodles boiled in savory broth,
and garnished with crisp slivers of green onion.
Sushi will become your bread and butter.
You'll want to stir-fry all the time.
You'll eat peanut sauce like catsup.
Your skin will smell like curry steeped
in coconut milk with onions.
You'll eat it all, over and over,
until even your tears
taste like ginger.

3

My Husband Is Burning

He doesn't seem to know
that smoke is rising from his left hand.
His whole right arm engulfed in flames
continues to hold his cell phone to his ear
until his beard is crackling.
He goes to work like this.
He comes home and parts of him are gone.
Still, he is on the phone,
now holds it in the crook of his neck,
to confirm his weekend job while
his feet are turning to ash.
He goes to fix his mother's garage door,
broken again, and his ear falls off.
Tonight, he tried so hard to hold me,
but there was nothing left—
charred socket for a shoulder,
not even a stub for an arm.

Sonnet for a Husband

You are the hero, eager to make right our world on fire,
ready to catch the robin's egg before it hits the ground.
This is how you love, by rescue and by relief.
But need is a stock character, an unintended thief,
like a cow bird in a bluejay's nest pushes out one egg.
If you play the hero, then I am the distressed maiden.
A tiny thing, newly slicked unable to feed itself.
How it cries and cries and teeters on survival alone.
And if these are the roles, who is the villain in our play?
Who will put on the penetrating eye and candid tongue?
Without truth, we are fools pleasing no one and everyone.
Sometimes I'd like to be the hero of my own crisis,
rescue myself from myself in the third act, just in time.
Then I would be the giver and the taker all at once.

Why I Lose Rings

Left behind again and again,
my desk at work, beside the kitchen sink,
a record of every place I've been.
It can't be helped, it isn't natural—
the constant moist skin underneath wants out,
the diameter as wide as all the things I ought to be.

But I was born in a year that was ruled by wood,
and metal cuts wood.
I've seen it before,
a tree grown over the chain around its waist—
a chain for hanging,
a chain for yanking you out,
roots naked, twitching in the air.

How to Divide One Whole You

1/3 parent + 1/3 employee + 1/3 spouse
does not equal one whole you but
permutations of you.
Only one can execute its function
at any given time.

Requirements call for
1 ½ parent you + 1 ½ work you + 1 ½ spouse you =
invalid calculation. Insufficient source.
Multiply by a factor of
school concert x illness x hosting holiday =
exponentially negative integer you.
Divide this number by
the number of your children,
given age as a factor of x.

Write a proof that demonstrates
One you — job + bills = increase in sanity?
Or 1/3 parent you — cleaning toilets — cooking =
increase in you?

You are the product of division.
You ÷ x = disappearing you,
reduced to null, an imaginary unit,
when all you want is to be prime,

divisible by only one and yourself.
But 0 too can be divided by any number
and still remain the same.

My Life in a Purse

I carry the past tucked in a zippered pocket,
small scrap of *I love you, Mommy*
on the back of used paper—
some unrelated picture-piece,
the whole long ago scattered,
unidentifiable.

I carry confidence in a tube
of lipstick, and comfort
in a tube of Tylenol.
Well-being in a small pouch
full of Band-Aids to cover any
accidental disappointments, insults.
And next to it I keep pleasure,
each piece wrapped in shiny paper—
sweetness on the tongue
to overtake the bitter.

And I carry my heart which buzzes and glows
with notifications, sometimes just to say
on this day six years ago…
Do you remember?
Sometimes my heart rings and
I answer—worried that my heart is sick
or in trouble. I ask if it's ok.
Lately it never calls just to chat
or ask how my day is going.

But this is how it is between
me and my heart.
With me everywhere I go
but far away.

Maybe the purse is too small for my heart,
or my heart doesn't have enough
to keep itself illuminated
for so long.
My heart wants its own life,
deep and roomy—
full of things it carries
for itself.

4

When We Come Back to Town, We Come Back to the Body

Small network of streets,
avenues like arteries,
each house an organ that shudders and pumps.
People flow out and back,
small cells that fetch and earn,
serve and desire,
want and must cresting and retreating all the time.
Small things carried on a tide.

The heart is both master and servant,
and we are the servant of the servant,
the ruler and the worker, tethered.
When we come back to town,
we follow its paths,
searching for the missing, the familiar—
the tree on the corner a birthmark,
the red bricks of the school a scar.
We come back again and again,
thrumming with urgency
for some things to have changed,
to revise the story to be anything
other than it actually was.

Observing the Narcissist in Its Natural Habitat

It lives alone but depends on others.
Preys on the fatty self-esteem
of the old and young
over a vast hunting ground—
workplaces and social events.
It lives in a seasonal climate
of admiration and pity,
comes out of its deep rocky burrow hungry
for attention.

It will never share
or mate with other narcissists.
It will eat its young.
Those who escape will travel miles away,
make their own burrows
with a fifty-fifty chance
of becoming a narcissist.

But the adaptation can be seen
when it lowers its head,
howls out of starvation.
Once, it was a species like others—
scoured the ground for love rooted and sprouting
beneath the brush, enough love fallen
from the trees
to sustain them all.

Homemade Dress, 1971

My mother made it
with a zipper across its empire waist,
below the breast
so she could easily feed us, her innovation
and intelligence stitched together.
This dress wanted to travel, to become,
to hear others say, *You are a valuable dress*.

But my mother, poor, exhausted,
forgot to zip up. Her determination
accidentally spilled out as she hung the laundry.
Baby after baby mewled on this dress
for years, an idea whose hemline broke,
made from the fabric of adaptation
now pilled over,
made to hold the value of herself so close.
Older than me, I wear it now,
feed my own children from its zippered form.

A Revisionist's Dream of Ice Cream

It struck us overnight, like a cold sweat
and an ache deep in our bones.
Our bellies rumbled;
we began to eat it every day,
sometimes twice.
We ate it in the car while it rained and
our thighs stuck to the seat. Sometimes,
we let it melt and drank it
while it eased into our bellies like mother's milk.
We fed it to the dog.
When we dreamed, our fingers twitched.
We ate it in our bed. It cooled us
like a washcloth during fever.
We languished in delirious visions—
a childhood revised
with all the things we ever wanted.

Eating My Korean

It's because I never bowed to my parents
on New Year's when I was young.
I have forgotten why
we take off our shoes in the house.
Because I wore white to my wedding,
but in Korea it's a color for funerals—
to honor the soul not the state
of your reproductive organs. This is why

I can't make a flavorful *bibimbop*,
can't sauté the fiddlehead *gosadi*
the right medium, neither soggy nor crisp,
or balance the ratio of sesame oil to rice just so.
Can't roll *geem bop* tight and firm.
Why I can't eat spicy.

If I eat a steady diet of Korean,
would it trigger a metamorphosis?
All fermented *kimchi* in the legs.
Pickled baby garlic, dried squid in the arms.
If I marinate perilla leaves in soy sauce,
wrap rice and meat in red lettuce,
dip everything in *gochujang*,
would random strangers still ask
if I'm Chinese, Japanese,
maybe Filipina?

If I ensure every guest leaves my home
with pears or persimmons, truly learn
this simultaneous thanks and apology for their time,
would I suddenly speak the language
of my ancestors, by instinct know
which word shows proper respect,
which gesture is called for?
To stick your chopsticks straight up
in a bowl of rice is only for the dead.
The word to say *goodbye* if you are leaving
different from the word to say *goodbye*
if you are being left.

If I brine this knowledge,
bury it in a clay *onggi* for the winter
in the soil of my heart, maybe then
my roots would taste robust, familiar, and mine.

Flavor Is in the Hands

They know a ripe avocado is not like
the firm baseball of a closed heart, or
a brother's finger pressing
into the flesh of your arm.
Soft as a hand holding your hand.

Or just the right spot to break
the asparagus spear
where structured meets mutable.
They know to keep kneading the dough
if it stretches and tears
like bending the rules. Know when
to be bold and when to stop
before it's tough and tight.

They can find a way
with what's on hand.
Garlic semi-sticky on the fingers?
Crush it open instead,
with the handle of your knife,

where to hold it so that it floats
balanced, finishing quick but even,
flat knuckles of one hand as a guide,
an extension of us, us guiding us.
The skin too is an organ that teaches

finely minced advice
told through scarred loops and whorls.

The mouth depends on the hands, while
the eyes tell you only what they want to see.
As for the nose, its flair for nostalgia
gets in the way, and the ears too passive
to create.

But the hands shape and mend.
They are the makers.
They guide you through the dark.

5

I Go Back to the Night I Was Named

Newborn baby on your father's belly,
curled comma of addition, you are also
the separator of the *I*.

The father from the Hollywood dreamer
in a third-world country.
Cobalt shirt, with yearning written
in the pattern of oil stains
divided from red Converse American prize
stitched with possibilities.
Borders now closed, each of these
a small state in the country of remorse.

But the name, oh the name,
with only three letters as a map.
Take my advice.
Expectation is an uncharted darkness,
and hope holds many names.

Yours is the one
you will answer to when called.

Lessons in Chess

On a battlefield I mounted my strategy—
steadied the knight's horse, and culled
the backward pawns fallen behind.
I pushed to advance—
low infantryman pushing through
calculus tests and chemistry labs
on unknowns, a way to advance
one square forward to win
the match.

I avoided closed positions
at home, hemmed in by friendly pieces—
friendly fire, artillery of unhappiness.
All the pieces trying to save themselves.
On the board there was danger everywhere;
a person could not rest.
I envied the rook that stayed in place
as an escape. Only it could castle with the King,
switch places if it followed the rules,
become a prized piece
protected by the other pieces.
Until I saw it was a sacrifice.

But then I learned new ways
to get the lowest piece across the board—
how to Queen the pawn.
Sixteen-year-old me transformed.

I became a master of deflecting attack,
holding my own ground,
how to escape entrapment from
a forced position.
I was free to move any direction,
any number of spaces—
the strengths of all the pieces
combined.

I learned to clear the center squares—
from there the Queen dominates.
More powerful than the King,
I learned to let her rule the board.

What You Learn to Say in French

You learn to link one small sound to another
after another, into a train gathering speed.

You learn how to press the tip of your tongue
against the back of your teeth, and say
to your older brother, that you've watched him—
because speaking requires watching.
You've heard his footsteps late at night,
and the front door close softly behind him.

You learn how to round your mouth,
like blowing a small ring of smoke,
and say to your mother
that her love is like eating
one small potato
all day.

Driving Lessons for Girls

You'll get there faster if
you stay in your lane—
even if there's stop and go,
let momentum carry you forward.
Look one hundred feet ahead for the signals.
Glide in easy, no need to brake
until the end is kind of smooth.

Even though you want to floor it
when the light turns green, watch
for the left turns across your path.
You don't always benefit from being first.
Set your own pace.
Let anyone in a rush pay the price.

Watch your tires—they keep you grounded,
give you traction against conditions ahead.
If it's flat, you're strong enough
to lift the solution out and fix the problem.
If you're stuck, don't keep spinning your wheels—
try something different.

Let the carburetor draw air deep and circulate.
If the heart of your car is stressed,
let the engine pump a low steady rhythm.
Listen to your car. It'll tell you
when something ain't right, a sign of need—

hum and whir a cough or ache.
It'll carry you wherever you want to go
if you take care of it.
Don't matter if the body is shiny, decked out—
make sure the insides are good.

Get lost and find your way again. Learn
where the roads will lead.
Read the signs to decide
which fork to take.
And never, ever
let a stranger drive your car.

He Said He Knew of a Place Where We Could Swim

So the three of us squeezed into the front
of his unfamiliar truck.
Every time he shifted,
his hand darted out to brush my thigh
quick and whole,
like a big fish eating a little fish.
We drove a while,
waiting to be let out
to see the sun still warming
the wide flat smoothness of rocks.

When we finally dove into the water,
it was cold as metal on our skin.
But he was like water
caressing my waist, and
drawing my sister's hair into a point
down her back.
So we kept on diving,
deeper and deeper, dark places
where the living don't stay.

When he called to us with a rope
cut long enough to bind,
we didn't know
the bones of fish were near those rocks.
We didn't know
how cold the rocks could get.

How Much to Cut

When you make the first cut, be open,
attuned, because each curl is asking
for its own direction, and who are we
to deny them independence?

Be gentle with each strand that shines slick
and brown, as you pull it even.
They glow red in the sun,
like viewing light through closed eyelids,
watching the heart pump joy and sorrow
through its vessels.

And be selective. I know
this is an act of survival, an amputation
of the unhealthy.
But each strand is a lesson layer upon layer,
and all I have learned
has seeped from my body there.

Listen carefully as we discuss how much to cut.
Sever only the bad habits and useless tics,
unhappy memories dried and split.
Cut past all the unmendable
broken ends.

Every Morning, I Slip My Feet into My Feet

My fingers stretch out the fingers.
I roll up the long gloves of my arms
and zipper myself up. I walk around—
my mouth all day is cautious
what it lets out, what it yearns for.
The perfect glass of my eyes lets in some light,
sometimes enough
I become transparent, illuminated, dark
blotches of the past bloom
underneath, my mother a blue vein above my ankle,
my father a floret on my arm.

When I come home,
I want to let my skin rest, lay it down,
cover it with a cool sheet of forgiveness.
If I pamper it like a thousand-dollar dress,
keep it out of the sun to avoid fading,
blot any stains from spilled opinions,
I can let the muscle and bone be naked.
I can imagine the ways
it will stretch if I change, then hope
it will never become too loose
to hold me all together.

As You Drive by the Cornfield on County Road 522

It flickers like an old movie
all the way from 1953. The corn unwithers
to wax ripe and milky sap,
the farmhouse rebuilds itself, caved-in
corner of the roof shores up
broken porch beams mend their splintered ends,
and paint brightens to linen white.
Lights turn on, and silhouettes walk by
the windows, a clairvoyant dream
made thick inside by all the people
dressed in black who cross themselves.
Someone has died and dies over and over
each time you pass by like
peaches falling every season.
But this is not your memory, not your story.
This movie plays on repeat
gives no reason why, no telling for who.

You learn the plot, the characters—
the man on the porch, the uncle,
calls for his dead brother's son
with his fedora and one cupped hand
an amplified temporary almost heart.
The boy stays low in the field,
one eye, between the stalks, sees
the sharp creases of his uncle

snap in the wind, like a flag,
like a sign of last hope.

You find reasons to drive by
roll down your window to hear it,
the uncle calling and calling.
You pull over, sit for hours—
you want to know how it ends,
prove we can survive what happens,
but over and over it plays out the same.
You can never find an answer.
You can never know the end.

6

A Poem for No One

—after Charles Wright's "It's Sweet to Be Remembered"

                This is a poem for   no one,

But   is remembered

by   every child   much longer

than any   fairy or saint,   than

                any secret hidden beneath   a rock

or   any wound   is remembered.

               If you grow troubled,
               lay your thoughts   beside
the discarded objects   along   the road.

             Let any dog come   if he's lucky

            clean the bones   or
                  follow   some tune
         to piss on a graveyard of troubles   or

gnaw on a   harsh word

to be ground up and never   uttered.

            Let them stay buried   in childhood

where they might   churn to fertile dirt   or

                     grow something sweeter   back

Only then let them   spread leaves   in the day.

-

You've been dreaming about street lamps again

before the same strange house,
many nights in a row.
And a light begins to stir in your belly that says
you were on this street before, but
they called it by another name.

It shows you the turned-up stone where you once fell
and your blood left a small horseshoe of a stain.
It shows you the hundreds of people who have lived
in that house, and walked over the stones
until the stones became smooth.

And from each of their bellies,
there's a burning, soft glow too,
that calls to the light in your belly.
Calls it by name. They discuss you,
how those streetlamps are burning for you.

In the Kingdom of Obsolete Things

In the Kingdom, there is no ruler.
There are no rules.
Just an increasingly crowded land
of unwanted things.
Everybody knows someone who arrived before.
In the kitchen section of town, they come every season:
garlic dicer, lemon zester,
one unfortunately named soul—vegetti.
No one wanted to say
spaghetti squash was just a trend.

The blender resents the food processor,
who took his place. And they all laughed
when the slow cooker arrived in town. He thought
he could beat that Instapot and would've,
but they broke his lid.

In the technology section
iPhone 5 is jealous of iPhone 8.
With GPS, it could have found its way in the world.
But the new generation still became the old.
Phone cases mated to each discarded phone like a spouse,
meant only for each other—'til death do them part—
while charging cords and plug heads mourn
for their lost mates.

There are only two ways out of the Kingdom—
a second life, in a new place—
they might be made whole again.
The other a place of bodies crushed or melted,
they become a dismantled collection.
When the humans come with an empty box,
they pray in the language of watts and amps,
their cords pressed together in supplication.
When empty spaces are made,
they curse the can opener in the dark
for his secret, his talent,
how he could always be of use.

This Morning, While Washing the Dishes

I was still in our kitchen, but not our kitchen.
The clock became a calendar
with a painted cow.
Someone had noted an appointment on the 10th,
and circled it.
The cereal was in a different place.
There were ripe persimmons in the refrigerator,
a firm golden orange I'd never seen up close.
And on the refrigerator door
was the photo of a girl I didn't recognize.
But the small bow shape of her lips was my lips.
The plump round apple cheeks were your cheeks.

How Best to See the Stars at Night

Go far away from other people.
Their lights wash out what is around you,
illuminate their own direction.
Find the horizon of your present where
the tall buildings and trees of your life
nowhere obstruct your view, the air
around you ink black enough
to block out your own body.

The stars know who they are—
the world turns, the stars remain in place.
The Water Bearer, The Virgin, The Archer,—
the constellations cycle through the sky
in their own seasons, a window
to find yourself in outline,
a sky map of you.

Measure the distances between
your failures and achievements,
nebulae of things you've left undone,
small grains of cosmic dust
burning up in the atmosphere
in the doctor's office one afternoon
as the oncologist removes a scraping of you
the size of a star, a dot in the sky,
an entire sun somewhere dying,
growing cold, a universe of stars. Your body

sinks into the exam table.
See it, all the light
still travelling years and years
after the star has gone dark.

Ways to Be Buried in the Movies

In a ten-thousand-dollar casket,
titanium shell lined with satin—
as if you might feel
uncomfortable in anything less.
Or as a root ball—food for a peach tree,
pieces of you in each ring, each fruit bud
growing fat and sweet. The peaches
will taste like you.

Or set adrift in a burning boat
your charred remains coming ashore
in some unexpected place.
(Would this violate law?)
May there always be two coins over your eyes
to pay the toll as you cross,
and your sword in both hands
upon your chest.

Perhaps in a white cotton gown,
your face covered by muslin to deter the flies
(as if you might feel the flies),
pestering you before they set you ablaze
on a pyre (do this
in the appropriate country where
they do not burn heroes and heretics
the same way—standing up, alive).

No one ever wants a movie in which
you are unceremoniously reduced to ash
in an industrial oven, mixed
with the remnants of other people
then scattered near the places you lived:
the supermarket, the gym,
the corners of buildings that catch the leaves
where the dust of you circles
with a plastic bag and empty wrappers.
Or at the park where you are churned
by the feet of all the dogs
who piss on you.

Give us the glamour of a Hollywood death,
an ending to look forward to.
Anticipation is for the living,
not the dead.

After We Buried
the Dog in the Dark

He came back. I saw him
in the grass, the white of him
glowing in the floodlight,
the wind turning it off and on again.
I saw his face at the door,
waiting to be let in,
his nose leaving smears across the glass.
Days later, I heard him in the kitchen
pacing blindly for his supper
and that night a soft crinkle
as he shifted in his bed.

Love wants to be fed.
It will return again and again,
holding a memory firmly in its jaw,
and you must throw or keep.
It will grow old,
too weak to walk.
You'll carry it everywhere at the end
until it nods, turns in a circle,
lies down.

Acknowledgments

The Apple Valley Review: "Broken Umbrella Song," "He Said He Knew of a Place Where We Could Swim," "A Revisionist's Dream of Ice Cream"

Bacopa Literary Review: "Flavor Is In the Hands, "Homemade Dress, 1971"

Cider Press Review: "All Your Lives, Your Sister and You Wore Long Braids"

Faultline: "My Husband Is Burning"

Flywheel Magazine: "Why I Lose Rings"

Gyroscope Review: "Observing the Narcissist in Its Natural Habitat"

Laurel Review: "I Was Born in a Room With Only Four Seats," "When We Come Back to Town, We Come Back to the Body"

Painted Bride Quarterly: "That Time You Stole Someone's Shopping Cart"

Philadelphia Stories: "Lust," "You've Been Dreaming About Streetlamps Again"

A Smartish Pace: "I Go Back to the Night I was Named"

The Sun: "After We Buried the Dog in the Dark"

"What You Learn to Say in French" was published in *Challenges for the Delusional I,* ed. Christine Malvasi (Jane Street Press, 2012).

"I Go Back to the Night I was Named" was reprinted in *More Challenges for the Delusional II,* eds. Ona Gritz and Dan Simpson (Diode Editions, 2018).

"After We Buried the Dog in the Dark" was featured on the podcast *The Slowdown* on August 11, 2023.

"He Said He Knew of a Place Where We Could Swim" received the 2009 Editor's Prize from *Apple Valley Review.*

About the Author

Jin Cordaro received her MFA from Fairleigh Dickinson University. Her work has been featured on the podcast *The Slowdown* and has appeared in *The Sun, Painted Bride Quarterly, Faultline,* and *Bacopa Literary Review,* among others. She is the recipient of the Fairleigh Dickinson Director's Award, a grant finalist from the Sustainable Arts Foundation, and the recipient of the Editor's Prize from *Apple Valley Review*. She currently calls central New Jersey her home, where she enjoys life with her family.

www.ingramcontent.com/pod-product-compliance
Lightning Source LLC
Chambersburg PA
CBHW060538080526
44586CB00012B/782